Staying Warm

by Maryellen Gregoire

Consultant:
Adria F. Klein, Ph.D.
California State University, San Bernardino

capstone
classroom

Heinemann Raintree • Red Brick Learning
divisions of Capstone

Some places are very cold.

Staying warm is good for your health.

Humans use hats and coats to stay warm.

Polar bears live
in a very cold place.

Thick fur keeps them warm.

Arctic foxes live in very cold places.

Thick fur keeps them warm.

They cover their noses to protect them from the cold.

Muskrats stay warm in icy water.

Muskrats grow a double layer of fur to stay warm.

A harp seal lives on snow and ice.

Blubber under its skin keeps it warm.

Penguins live in a very cold place.

Feathers and fat keep them warm.

There are many ways to stay warm when it is cold!